10 EXTRAORDINARY LESSONS
from an
Ordinary Dad

A father's life saving impact through simple words

Carlos J. Avent

One 6 Four Media, LLC
Baltimore, MD, U.S.A.

Copyright © 2018 Carlos J. Avent & One 6 Four Media, LLC

All rights reserved. No part of this book may be reproduced or used in any manner without the prior written permission of the copyright owner, except for the use of brief quotations in a book review.

To request permissions, contact the publishing owner of One 6 Four Media at carlosjavent@outlook.com.

ISBN: 978-0-578-20607-3
First edition: June 2018

Edited by: One 6 Four Media, LLC
Cover art by: Chandana Prasanna
Layout by: One 6 Four Media, LLC

Forewords

"10 Extraordinary Lessons from an Ordinary Dad is an inspirational read from start to finish. The lessons within are universal, and they can be felt and related to by people of all walks of life. Regardless of one's relationship with their father or lack thereof, I highly recommend reading this work from Carlos J. Avent, soaking up the lessons and passing them on to future generations."

Matt Prestbury – *Founder of Black Fathers, Inc.*

"It's so refreshing to see a book focus on the needed narrative of the power and beauty of Black fatherhood. I'm a daddy's girl and my dad has always been there so this book quickly drew me in. Dad's play a vital role in not just their child's life but they are pertinent role models and pillars of our communities. A father's strength, dedication,

love and vulnerability to his family should be displayed. Thank you Carlos for authentically telling the story of what it is to be a Black King raising Black royalty."

Kelsey Nicole Nelson – *Award-winning Journalist, Media Personality & Philanthropist*

"Carlos J. Avent is a young lion with the wisdom of his elders...I not only enjoyed this book, but I know he will be a thought leader on these issues for years to come."

Marc Clarke – *TV/Radio/Media Personality, Author*

"As a single mom raising a son in today's world, I am so inspired by this book! The chapter entitled "You only have one mother" speaks to my heart and soul. Carlos captures the Extraordinary Lesson of respecting one's mother and valuing women masterfully! I know this book will be my go-to guide for helping my young prince grow healthily into a young man. 10 Extraordinary Lessons from an Ordinary Dad will be a lamp unto my son's feet and a

light unto his path as he begins his journey into adulthood."

Tori Rose, *The Connector* **– CEO of THEOO, LLC**

"This is a very thought provoking, relatable, and most importantly, a needed book. We live in a day and time where so many dismiss the idea of the importance of black fatherhood. This book speaks to that and so much more."

Micah Butler – Podcast Host, *Convos for the Culture*

Carlos Avent's book is an engrossing memoir as well as an inspirational guide to becoming an honorable citizen and caring father. In recounting the impact of conversations he had with his father throughout his childhood, Carlos tracks his moral development as he receives the life lessons his father imparts. Written with deep perspective and self-knowledge, Carlos approaches his subject with clear-eyed affection and respect for his father's efforts to instill important values. Carlos' gratitude to his father shines through, even as his recognizes his shortcomings and is a refreshing antidote to the spate of nonfiction books that chronicle childhood grievances. The book brims with grace and gratitude as it introduces us to Carlos' strong and mature voice and the wisdom earned from his ancestors.

Gina Lobaco, *Nonprofit Consultant*

Chapters

~~~~~~ ∞ ~~~~~~

Let **ME** Explain... 1

"YOU **Only Have ONE** *Mother.*" 6

"**Them** boys **AINT your friends.**" 26

"Nah **I'll be AT WORK.**" 42

"*Lemme' get* 2-4-3 **FIFTY/FIFTY BOX.**" 56

"**Same thing,** *different name.*" 68

"You gotta *think three moves* **ahead.**" 80

"**OPEN** your mouth and **speak!**" 92

"**Nothing beats a fail** *but a* **TRY.**" 102

"**I'm your DADDY, but** *He's your Father.*" ... 114

"**Be BETTER than me.**" 126

THE EPILOGUE: **Every** *story* has *an*
origin 134

ABOUT the ***Author*** 141

Let **ME** *Explain*...

"What made you want to write that?"

"Who is it supposed to be for?"

"What are you hoping happens with this?"

I heard those questions often around the beginning of 2018. Those three questions, in no particular order, would come up every time I'd share with others that I was writing a book titled, '10 Extraordinary Lessons from an Ordinary Dad'. Sometimes the questions would come with enthusiasm, other times with criticism. That would depend on who I was talking to at the time. But regardless of such, my answers remained the same then, and they remain the same as you read this.

I value the presence, advice, and guidance that a father bestows upon a child. The lessons that I learned from my father were too valuable not to share. So, I often thought of those who may not have been as fortunate as I was to have a father that was so present and giving. I thought about those whose fathers were absent for whatever reason, and those who have now become a father or even those women who have unfortunately found themselves raising a son on their own and need some foundational guidance.

As I spent many nights after work, up until 3am writing this book, I would envision those different people sitting across the table from me, who would be in need of those "Dad lessons" that they probably thought only existed on TV with dad's from sitcoms. The likes of James Evans from Good Times, Phillip Banks from the Fresh Prince of Bel-Air, or Carl Winslow from Family Matters. I wanted to bring that type of dad to life for those who need it, those who want it, and those who should see the impact that a father's presence and guidance can have. I wanted to show that the type of love and lessons from a father who cares and who is present, doesn't only live on TV or with a father that's famous or hold some sort of prestigious title in life. My father was an ordinary dad. He was an everyday joe, blue-collar working man who in his own simplistic yet stern way, save my life. So, it became my hope that I could pass on his wisdom, his lessons, and my perspective and it possibly save someone else's life.

So to answer the questions…

That's why I wrote it, that's who I wrote it for, and that's what I'm hoping happens when it's all said and done.

Take a journey through my experiences.

"You **Only** *Have* **ONE** *Mother.*"

Dad: *So why did you be hard-headed and leave the porch when your mother told you to stay your butt on the porch?*

I'm sitting there, at the dining room table in the seat to the left of Dad, who always sat at the head of the table. I'm trying to look everywhere and anywhere I can, except for Dad's face. Why? Because I can feel him staring at me as he waits for an answer that's acceptable. I'm literally looking at the microwave knob, the scar on my right hand, the Lord's prayer on the wall, you name it. In my mind, I'm toggling between being both angry and fearful, knowing that a whoopin' was all but guaranteed at this point.

In my six-year-old mind, all I can think about is how unfair this is and how I'm always in trouble for something so stupid. The things I seemed to always be in trouble for, felt as if they were rules and consequences solely designed to keep me from having fun. I just wanted a level of freedom my other friends had. I was convinced that their lives were care-free, and mine was the one that was restricted. I felt restricted as if I had a ball and chain locked around my ankle. I didn't understand why I had to ask to do simple things like go to the store, go down the street to my cousin's house, or stay outside past the time when the streetlights came on.

Ok, back to the dining room table.

So, I sat there, wishing that I could be anywhere else but right there as Dad stared at me waiting impatiently for an answer. I would've preferred to be in school, church, Rite Aid, or almost anywhere but that dining room table at the time. At the top of my 'anywhere but here in this moment' list, I wished I could have been at Big Ma's house.

At this point, I've mustered up enough courage to answer my father. But it wasn't what he expected.

Me: *I wish Big Ma was my mother.* [as tears roll down my face because now, I feel like my parents hate me].

Why did I say that? Easy answer.

Big Ma was my paternal grandmother who lived about 10-15 minutes away from our home behind the Bus station. Some of my favorite cousins were always there often, especially in the summertime. I got to spend a good amount of time at Big Ma's house in the summer and being there with my cousins made me feel like I was "free" to do what I wanted. If I wanted Frosted Flakes in the afternoon loaded with extra sugar, no problem. If I wanted to go down to the next block to play basketball with the neighborhood kids, have at it. If I wanted to watch cartoons instead of being forced to watch the Young & the Restless in the middle of the day, it's all good, take the remote! As a kid, Big Ma's house was a place you wanted to be, you looked forward to going to and you hated to leave. I'm sure my cousins can attest to this.

Don't get me wrong. Big Ma didn't just let us run amuck. She was already in her seventies at this point, so her days of strict discipline were behind her. Her main focus was making sure we ate, didn't get sick, and were safe. Everything else was free game.

Back to the dining room table and the bomb I just dropped on my dad. So, he says this...

Dad: [slight sigh and empathetic stare] *Listen to me, don't you ever let your mother hear you say that. Big Ma loves you and I know you love being over there. But no one will love you like your mother. Your mother gave birth to you, and she loves you very much., she loves you more than anyone else in this world ever could. How would you feel if she wasn't here? What if you were like some of these other kids who wish they had a mother like yours? You ever think of that? I don't care what she does that you may not like or be upset about, she does it for your own good.* ***You only have one mother****...just one. Don't you ever forget that.*

Never in my six-year-old life had I ever felt so misunderstood. As much as I thought I had made matters worse for myself, to my surprise, Dad just told me to get up, go upstairs and apologize to my mom for what I've done and to give her a hug.

After wiping my eyes and trying to restore my voice, I left the dining room table to do what I was told. I was ok with it because this meant that the whoopin' might be off the table.

I get to the top of the stairs and begin what seemed like at that time, the longest walk down the hallway ever to my mom's room. As I'm walking up to her door, I'm rehearsing in my mind how I'm going to just quickly do this and go on about my day. I get to the room and my mom is there in her usual spot on her side of the bed. As I get ready to say what I was told to say, I instantly became overwhelmed with the thought of life if she weren't here. That very statement from my father kept playing repeatedly in my head. It had gotten to the point where I was upset with myself for putting myself in this situation and furthermore, thinking about how I made my mother feel.

I couldn't get out what I was trying to say because I was fully engaged in a crying spell. I just wanted to hug her, figuring my hug would say what I needed to say for me. That moment gave me a renewed perspective on my relationship with my mother and helped me to realize that she wasn't just here to stop me from having my six-year-old fun. I didn't quite understand the correlation between love and telling me that I had to stay on the porch, but I didn't care to question it any further. I also had a lot of time to reflect on it because Dad took away my toy chest for a week.

I guess I had that coming.

~~~~~ ∞ ~~~~~

Dad: *What happened today?*

Me: [in a teary shaken voice] *nuffin.'*

Dad: *Welp, that's not what your mother told me. Now I'm gon' give you another chance to tell me the truth..*

Me: [attempting to not cry] *Ma said I could go outside…… and that I had to stay on the porch.*

Dad: *Ok and?! What else? I know that wasn't it.*

Me: *I stayed on the porch but then we started playing tag and I forgot… but I was still in front of the house.*

Dad: *What did your mother tell you to do?*

[Making a very conscious effort to not cry, but it's not working. My eyes are watery at this point.]

Me: *Stay on the porch.*

It might have been over that day, but that wouldn't be the last time that I would hear Dad say, *"you only have one mother."*

[12 years later…]

Dad: *Your mother is upset with you.*

Me: *Why? Because of the trash? I don't like taking it out at night….*

Dad: *Nope.*

Me: *Well why then? What did I do now?*

[very irritated at this point]

Dad: *What time did you come in last night?*

Me: *It was about 1:30[am]. That wasn't too late the movie ended at like 12:45[am]. I told her that.*

Dad: *Ok when did you tell her that?*

Me: *Right before I left out at 6[pm]. I'm not seeing what's wrong here…*

Dad: *You told her that before you left and that was the last time she heard from you.*

Me: *So?? It's not like I stayed out all night or just didn't come back home.*

Dad: *That's not the point.*

Me: *Then what is? I don't get this man...*

Dad: *You're right you don't get it. You don't watch the news; it's so much happening out there in the world son and your mother worries about you every time you step out that door. She doesn't sleep peacefully until she hears from you. She sits up and worry. I told you before and I'm tellin' you again.... When you leave out it is not gonna hurt you to pick up that phone and just call and say, "Ma I'm ok I'm doing this and that and I'll be home soon." That's it. Won't take you any time at all to do that.* **You only have one mother** *son, don't leave her up all night worrying about you when all you gotta do is just call her and let her know you're ok. Got me?*

Me: *Yes sir.*

What could I say? Dad was right. I, like most young adult at the time, didn't watch the news. It was boring. It was that thing that "old people" did. At this time, cell phones weren't quite yet as advanced yet to provide me with the several options of newsfeeds 24/7, so I wasn't very well-informed of anything happening in the streets unless it was a hot topic talked about with some friends. I was a 20-year-old young man, in college, with my own car, making my own money from working two part-time jobs that added up to full-time hours, and the best part, girls were finally giving a young brother some attention! So, in my mind, I'm a grown man, responsible, educated, and the last thing I need or should have to do, is check in with Mom to give an update on my comings and goings.

Wrong.

Having this conversation with Dad gave me a different perspective on what I was doing, how I viewed myself and what I was doing, and above all, how my actions impacted someone else.

Specifically with that "*someone else*" being my mother.

As grown and responsible as I believed that I was, it didn't relieve me of some harsh realities that I had ignored often. At this stage in my life, I had begun to experience friends falling victim to crime and gun violence. Though I wasn't oblivious to the perils of the streets of Baltimore, I always had a "*that won't be me*" attitude about it.

I won't get carjacked.

I won't go out on a date and be set-up by a girl who plotted to have me robbed, assaulted, or killed.

I won't be a victim of a spiked drink.

I won't be the one to take a stray bullet in a high-crime neighborhood with friends or a girl I like.

My car won't breakdown in a part of town that I'm not familiar with.

These things won't happen to me because I'm a good guy, I'm careful, I'm responsible and I mind my business.

Good enough, right?

These are the things that kept my mother up at night. These are the scenarios that played in her mind over and over as she would tell my dad to call me or ask him if he's heard from me. She would be nervous and anxious every time the house phone rung, hoping that it's me just calling to say, *"I'm ok and on my way home."* While at the same time, she would be dreading and praying it's not a police precinct or someone calling with bad news about her son. She would stay up for as long as her body would allow her, hoping that I would come walking through that door any minute now, and she could then at that point, peacefully sleep knowing that I was home.

At the time, I knew none of that. All I knew was that I was too cool, too grown, and too responsible to call and do some frivolous check-in.

To me, the idea of calling home to check-in was laughable. It was a sign of no independence, no freedom, or still being on a short leash. I couldn't imagine at the time, being on a date and having to say, "*let me call my mom and let her know I'm ok*." I hated doing it. I wanted to be everything that my friends expected me to be at 20 years old. Meanwhile, I was leaving my mother at home with four things to deal with:

Stress. Worry. Anxiety. Fear.

I left my mom with those four things to contend with every night that I went out at my own leisure or stayed out after work. All the while, I had the power to change that and ease her mind, but instead of just giving her a simple call, I chose not to. I instead chose that impressing my friends and showing that there was no short leash here, was more important. But I have to say, after Dad gave me that talk about Mom's perspective and what he sees and hears every time I'm out in the streets, it made sense, and it was humbling. The request was simple and deep down, I knew that. I just chose myself, selfishly.

I thank God that my mother never had to take a call from a police officer about me or a courtesy call from me in central booking, or worse, the call from the morgue needing someone to identify my lifeless body. For me, there was something about knowing someone else is losing sleep over you and your actions that can actually change your perspective on how you directly or indirectly respond to them and their request.

Especially when that person is your mother.

The Extraordinary Lesson: A mother's love knows no end.

The love of a mother is the precursor for how a man loves the woman in his life. As a boy grows into a young man and he learns how to love, and how to receive love from his mother, he becomes the gentleman that the right woman for him has longed for all of her life. She will appreciate him, be the best version of herself for him, be the life partner he never knew he needed, and build a life of love that last with him.

You may not notice this upfront, but your mother is the first woman to cherish your existence and own your heart. She is the first woman to care for you unconditionally. She is the first woman that shows you what love is supposed to feel like. She's the first woman to anticipate your needs before you say a word. She's the first woman to memorize how you like your food. She's the first woman to know how to encourage you when things are bad. Sometimes, especially early on, you might miss it, like I did. But know that her care, compassion, and love are the seeds that you need planted in your heart as you go through life. Those seeds are of the very same care, compassion, and love that she has unconditionally for you.

There is a common misconception that receiving love from your mother and showing love back to your mother makes you weak or a "Mama's Boy." That's because it has become synonymous with passive, dependent, and confrontational. I'm not sure who made that rule up, but when you're really a "Mama's boy," it's truly a testament to how you love and that you're emotionally present in relationships. When you understand this, along with understanding how this connects back to your mother's love, being called a "Mama's boy" takes on a totally different meaning. No longer will it be viewed as the spoiled type that view women as subservient beings who should wait on men hand and foot. Nor the type that is incapable of doing anything for himself much less leading in a relationship. But it takes on the meaning of being a standard of love to a woman who desires a love that exudes commitment, passion, and intimacy, from a man who leads with strength.

As a boy and later as a young man, my father made me realize that there will never be another one who love me like my mother. He also made me realize that it was my responsibility to reciprocate that love back to her because essentially, that's all she wants. When you do this correctly, the reward later in life is the distinction of becoming the gentleman for the right one. In a world full of bad boys, be the gentleman. The right woman will see you and no one but you.

There once was a man by the name of James Brown and he once wrote a song titled, "*This is a Man's World*". Great song, it was number one on the billboard R&B charts in 1966. However, the most important lyric in that song is, "*but it wouldn't be nothing, nothing, without a woman or a girl.*" If you truly think about your "world" and who's in it, then you will understand the truth behind that one line.

"Them boys AIN'T your friends."

~~~~~ ∞ ~~~~~

Dad: *I shouldn't have to keep coming up here, taking time off from my job because you don't know how to keep your mouth shut and do your work!*

Me: [silence]

Dad: *Should I?*

Me: *No sir.*

Dad: *Then why am I coming up here again?*

Me: *I dunno. I ain't do nuffin' but just talk to my friends. We were all talking but Ms. Barnes only seen me.*

Dad: *Who's we?*

Me: *Me, Brian, Paul, Anthony, and Arnold. The same people at my table.*

Dad: *What did I tell you 'bout them? Didn't I tell you learn to keep your mouth shut, do your work and stay away from them boys?*

Me: *Yes sir.*

Dad: *Then why can't you?*

Me: *We sit at the same table, and we weren't even talking loud.*

Dad: *I don't give a s**t what they do, I wanna know why you can't keep your mouth shut!*

Me: *[silence]*

Dad: *They talking to you to get you in trouble because they know they can. They don't care about you. Your real friends would say, 'aight Carlos be quiet let's pay attention'.* **Them boys ain't your friends***. You understand me?"*

Embarrassment. Confusion. Anger.

That's all I felt in that moment. Embarrassed that my father had to come to the school in the first place. Confused by at how he does not seem to understand why these are my friends and trying to understand what it is that he knows about them that I don't seem to know. Then there was the anger. Angry because I felt like my side of the story, my intentions, weren't being considered. This was just another one of those "dad thinks he has all the answers" moments for me. At 8-years-old, I was pretty sure that the days of having my dad dictate who my friends are were over. I could not figure out what gave Dad the right to choose my friends or tell me who can or can't be my friend? I'm the one who will see these guys every day whether at school or in the neighborhood. So, I should make that decision, right? So, I decided that I was going to ask him. I asked him why can't I be their friend?

Quickly I learned the answer to that was because he's my father, because he said so, and that was all that I needed to know.

When you're young, you're naïve. When you're young and naïve, you don't quite have the ability and aptitude to see ahead, to decipher, to see people for whom they are inside, and to see situations going bad before the first sign shows itself. None of that is quite developed yet, especially not at 8-years-old.

In other words, when you are young and naïve (or old and naïve... but that's a story for another day) you don't know it all as much as you like to believe you do. You live in the now. You live for today. You live to be accepted and liked. You live to trend on social media. Everything is a hashtag and right now fame. And if you're not careful, all of that will take priority in your life over the need to apply common sense and develop boundaries to support your discernment about those around you. A sad but true statement.

For me, I was that kid (minus the social media references because there was no social media when I was a kid). I just wanted to be accepted and liked. I realized that I already had a series of strikes against me.

- *I didn't get the cool haircuts like hi-top fades or low cuts with the part on the side.*
- *I didn't have name brand shoes and clothes like Nike, Jordans, or Ralph Lauren.*

- *I wasn't much of a young athlete. My coordination in sports was bad.*
- *I didn't get off the porch late into the night. That was a no-no.*

So, any time an opportunity presented itself that allowed me to feel like "one of the boys", it was an opportunity that was well worth taking to me. Even if it meant getting in trouble in class, getting a letter sent home or a phone call, or worse, in-school suspension. Why would I risk that knowing the kind of father I had to go home to? Simple. Because to me, trouble was attention. Attention was what I was seeking because in my thinking, the trouble that I was getting into, would change how I'm perceived. Then perhaps that would make me one of the cool kids, like the ones I call my friends.

However, Dad wasn't having it.

Dad seen it another way. He seen right through this flawed logic from a mile away.

All the while, he constantly reminded me that they aren't my friends.

At the core of it all, I just couldn't accept the fact that my dad knew more than me about my own friends. He knew more about them because to him, this was an all too familiar scene he had witnessed one too many times before. It's the scene where it starts off as petty, small infractions in school. Then, it leads to more mischievous activity that totes the line of breaking the law. Eventually, it ends up being nothing more than regrets or death. Or as he would say, "the grave or jail." So knowing that, Dad was overly cautious about who I hung with, who I called a friend, and who I learned from.

So, back to the friends who Dad said, "aren't my friends."

Dad was right. Each of those friends of mine were constantly in trouble and constantly getting notes sent home about their behavior. I knew I was a square when it came to them, but I wanted so badly to fit in and join this elite club of "coolness." Fast-forward 30 years, and it's unfortunate that I have to say that those same boys today are either dead, in jail, or have served significant jail time already. All of them in one way or another, became products or victims, of the street life. Drugs, guns, burglary, theft, kidnapping, just to name a few roads they've ended up on. Dad was protecting me from a future I couldn't see, a future I couldn't see and a future I didn't want. He didn't care how mad it made me to be a kid in the 90's, just looking to be accepted and liked. He cared about his son being alive 30 years later and not a product of the streets or a victim of circumstance. As a kid chasing acceptance, I couldn't see his efforts at the time. But being alive to tell the story later in life makes me appreciate his efforts.

In case you're wondering, the answer is "no."

No… that was not the only time or last time I had this type of conversation with Dad.

[4 years later]

Dad: *where you goin'?*

Me: *Outside. Gonna ride my bike up to Clifton Park.*

Dad: *Who you goin' with?*

Me: *Just me.*

Dad: *Who's gonna meet you there? I know you ain't riding up there by yourself.*

Me: *Oh just [insert friends' names]*

Dad: *When you start hangin' around them?*

Me: *I didn't really start, everybody is going up there, I just know they are too.*

Dad: *When you plan on coming back?*

Me: *Before it's dark for sure.*

Dad: *No, you're gonna be back before that. I want you back in the house by 6.*

Me: *But Dad it's already 4:16!*

Dad: *So?! What did I say?*

Me: *6. I just don't know why so early.*

Dad: *Because I don't want you hanging out too long with those boys.* **Them boys ain't**

your friends. They run these streets with the wrong crowd, and you aren't gonna be caught being with them when they decide to do some stupid s**t or do something and set you up to be blamed for it. You lucky I'm even letting you go. Be back in this house by 6 and I'm gonna call back to make sure you are.

At this point in time, I was able to understand Dad's point of view. I could see what he was trying to forewarn me about. However, I felt like since I was older and more mature now, that I didn't really need the warning. The boys whom Dad spoke of weren't all that bad in my opinion. Perhaps they would often just be out and about and fit the mold of your typical teen who spends all day and night in the streets. Sometimes being mischievous, other times just roaming about playing ball in this alley or rolling dice on the porch. To me, it represented something that I wanted…

Freedom and credibility.

I never noticed their parents telling them to be home before it got dark. Or if they did, they surely didn't care about obeying that direct order. However, what I really envied was the fact that those same boys seemed to always have money. Something I didn't have much of and I wanted to know how they did it. Did they have some sort of business? Maybe they were working under the table for somewhere and getting paid a lot to do the job? I never knew. But I was curious. So hanging around them was intriguing because I wanted in. Again, just like how I thought some years back, I wanted to appear as one of the "cool kids."

My vision was short sighted, Dad saw more about them than I could and could clearly see the road that they were traveling. Yet again, Dad was protecting me from something that I couldn't see for myself. The difference for me this time around was me feeling emboldened because I was mature and smart (according to me). So, I found no harm in rolling the dice on my father catching me or finding out that I went against what he said just to impress my friends.

What seemed to have always worked against me and any attempt to do something that I shouldn't be doing, was the fact that Dad knew everyone in the neighborhood, and I was often known as "Pop's son." Depending on who it was, "Pop's son" was the only name I had to them. With that working against me, the rebelling stage did not last long. This is when I decided to exercise some of that maturity I was so proud of and realize that the risk wasn't worth it.

It didn't take much for me to understand that sometimes it's just better to comply, for your own good and the good of your life. That too, was a lesson Dad gave me. Though I hated the strict rules and "short leash," I eventually trusted Dad more than chasing what I wanted. Or at least, what I thought I wanted.

The Extraordinary Lesson: Trust the wisdom of those who came before you.

Trusting my father's instincts and wisdom was hard. Often, it was a struggle because I wanted him to trust me to make the right decisions or that my decision was ok and nothing to worry about. I wanted to be trusted that I knew my friends more than he did. I wanted to be trusted that I could handle myself and roam the streets. I wanted to be able to do what I pleased, and be able to come back and say, "*see… told you. Nothing happened.*"

But I often forgot one important fact… that fact is that Dad had 31 years of experience in life over me already by the time he brought me into the world.

I had to come to the realization that between Dad and I, this wasn't a competition of experiences. This wasn't a place where I should challenge him. I needed to accept the fact that he knew better than I did or would. I struggled to accept that at times. Many times to be truthful about it. I just never wanted to believe that he was right, because to me, his right way didn't match up with my fun way. His right way made me look weak to my friends. His right way was causing me to lose the friends I wanted to have. When it came to who I associated myself with, the allure of being in the "in-crowd," accepted and fitting in, it just wasn't worth losing the confidence and trust of my father and above all, it wasn't worth losing my own way of life.

So essentially, his right way, was right all along.

It's unfortunate that now, some of the very ones Dad told me to stay away from, are either incarcerated, dead, or still living an edgy life trying to avoid one of the first two fates of our peers. When I visit the old neighborhood, I see more "R.I.P." messages marked in alleys or sidewalks that I care to see. I can go through and remember certain spots where friends were robbed, arrested or even killed. Then I have a 'What If?' moment …. What if I disobeyed Dad just once to prove that I can hang and do what I want? I'd probably be the forgotten behind one of these R.I.P. messages.

I'd confidently say now that those moments of being considered a square or whatever other name I was called for being a "good boy," probably and very likely saved my life. The more I seen these things happen, the more I realize that trusting his instinct and wisdom became the right thing to do.

"Nah I'll be AT WORK."

~~~~~ ∞ ~~~~~

Dad worked a lot. A lot of the time, he would be gone from sunup to sundown, and maybe a little longer. Each day consisted of his day job, then his part-time job at random places like evening shift building cleaning or shuttle driving. or simply

indulging in his side hustle, hacking *(That's a Baltimore thing for catching a ride with unofficial Lyft or Uber drivers).*

Because he worked so much, he missed a lot of track meets, family weekend outings, and band performances. Sometimes, he would be gone before I woke up. Sometimes, he wouldn't get back home until it was near time for me to go to bed. Afterwhile, it just became second nature to me. It was just meant to be expected and accepted that his work was his life and his contribution to taking care of his family.

Was I upset? Of course. I've had my days of wishing things were different. It wasn't long before I just channeled that emotion elsewhere. So, I started becoming occupied with other things so I wouldn't really think about it. But, when I did think about it, it really made me wish he were around more. Regardless of me knowing that working was his life.

Sometimes, I'd ask him anyway for some time together, even though I went into that conversation with the expectation of hearing the same answer.

[Wanting to play/learn Chess with Dad]

Me: *Dad can we play chess tonight?*

Dad: *Nah I'll be at work. Maybe Sunday.*

[Wanting Dad to see me at my track meet]

Me: *Hey Dad my track meet is at the armory this Thursday night. Are you off? Can you come?*

Dad: *Nah I'll be at work son. When's the next one?*

[Wanting to watch the Super Bowl with Dad]

Me: *Dad will you be home in time for the game? It starts at 6:20.*

Dad: *Nah I'll be at work 'til 9.*

[Going out with cousins, but need a ride from Dad]

Me: *They said I can go with'em if you can take me to meet them at their house.*

Dad: *Nah I'll be at work. If they can't come get you then I guess you ain't goin'.*

See… it never failed. Nine out of ten times, Dad had to work. At that time in my adolescent mind, all I wanted to know was why does work always seem to come before me or anything that I need? The answer to that seemed to be rather consistent to me. No matter the fact that I just wanted to spend time with my Dad, I can't because of work. Does he not get a day off? It was as if the norm was for him to come in from one job, then turn around and leave back out for another. And if he's off from one job, he goes to the other one asking for more hours that week or if he can come in early. Why? Enjoy a day off! More importantly, enjoy it with me!

I just wanted my Dad with me as much as possible. Like any other kid, I wanted to show my Dad off. I wanted that moment of saying, "*yeah that's my Dad there*". Also, having Dad around was a boost to my confidence. I felt like I could do anything when he was around to watch me or just be with me. Anything like climb on top of a garage and jump off at the end or run faster than Michael Johnson (Olympic gold medalist and former fastest man in the world). I felt protected and empowered. The more he had to work or was too busy to do things with me, the more I was torn between wanting him around and hoping that the next time I ask, that I'd get a "yes," and just simply being angry about it. Either way, I knew what it was, but I didn't understand why it was what it was…if that makes sense.

So, as I said before, it had eventually gotten to a point where I was no longer disappointed, and I accepted that this was just what Dad does. But it took some time to get there. It was definitely a process.

That process began the first time Dad took me to work with him. It came as a surprise, and I really didn't know what to expect. I'm not even sure if or how he knew I had gone from being bothered by us not being able to spend time together, to unfazed and withdrawn. Maybe he saw it on my face, or maybe my mother intervened again like she often did, I didn't care either way. The fact that I was going to spend time with Dad was good enough.

I was 11 years old the first time Dad took me to work with him. We caught two buses to get to South Baltimore, in the Fells Point area. Dad was the manager of the seafood department for a small local market called Foodtown in Fells Point. The journey began at 6:47am to get bus #1. We packed lunches, I had my drawing book with me in case I got bored, and I dressed warm because Dad said he goes in and out of the freezer a lot. I didn't care what Dad did with his day, I was just excited to be a part of it.

In that eight-hour day, I learned a lot about Dad that I had not known before. I learned first and foremost why he's slept until 1pm on his days off. More importantly I learned about his work ethic. It was as if I was seeing the man more than the father at home, but in a good way.

First, everyone knew him and liked him. It was almost as if he never had an enemy. If he did, he'd never let it be known. When he walked in, it was like a scene from the 80s sitcom, Cheers. Dad was like Norm and when he walked in, everyone shouts his name. This was when I learned that no one calls him by his name. He's "Pop" to everyone, or to some, "Mr. Pop." So, when he walks in, everyone goes, "Hey Pop!"

Also, he took work very seriously.

Everything was on a mental timer with Dad. Everything from how much time it takes to clock in, to how long it takes to walk from the freezer area to the produce walk-in fridge. Even how quick it is to restock the endcap of and set up the ice display. And of course, my favorite, how long it takes to walk to Taki's sub shop down the street for lunch.

The most important observation I made of Dad was how he approached his work with pride. He was particular about his display case and the presentation of the seafood section because it reflected not just his work, but himself as well. He acknowledged people right away and confidently, whether they were a customer or a co-worker. Often more times than not, he went the extra mile to help out. Again, because it was more than just about work, but it represented him as a person.

All of these little traits of character developed relationships that last beyond the job. This was a side of Dad I had not seen before, it was my first glimpse at a man and his work ethic and his personality. The more I observed him, the more I wanted to mimic him. A customer would come by and ask where something is, I would ask to show them myself. I tried to have the same eye for presentation as he did and understand the right time to restock so the case always looks fresh for customers. For me, this was a win-win-win. I was spending time with Dad, learning, and getting some rather tasty treats from the ladies in the bakery.

This went on for a few years, on and off. Mostly on weekends and during the summer sometimes until I was about 16. By that time, Dad wasn't bringing me to work with him as a "bring your child to work day" kind of moment. We actually became co-workers because he then asked Mr. Melvin (that was the boss) to hire me so I could earn money for my school needs (class ring, dues, prom, etc.).

The work ethic rubbed off on me eventually. I worked at the same store as my Dad as a stock associate. It was still an opportunity to spend time with Dad, but at the same time, I needed to earn my own money. Dad's work ethic taught me the sense of earning all that comes to me. Nothing is given. Also, truth be told, he just couldn't afford all of those expenses that come with high school, so this was the next best step.

Speaking of working to earn, this was also a time where Dad was rather vulnerable with me and let me see more than what I was used to seeing. During the early days of me going to work with him, I used to walk up to the cashier's office with him when he picked up his check. Then from there we'd walk down the street from his job to cash it at what I only knew to be called, the "cut-rate".

I watched the cashier give him bills that I had never seen before. Hundreds, fifties, a lot of twenties, and a few smaller bills. Then as we rode the bus back home, I asked Dad what he was going to buy with all of his money. I was hoping he'd say a car, but instead he immediately "shhh'd" me. Guess that meant it was a secret. So, I waited until we got home to ask again. Dad was upstairs in his room; he had his money spread out across the bed and in several piles. So, I asked again, "*Oooh Dad what you gonna buy?*"

Instead of being shhh'd this time, he decided to give me a glimpse into his world. He showed me where all his money was going. He first showed me a little piece of paper with a long list of names and amounts. These were people he had to pay back because he borrowed money from them during the week to keep food in the house, pay the gas & electric, pay the telephone company, or pay for something that I or my sisters or brother may have needed. Then there were some bills laid out that were past due. I was pretty good at doing quick math in my head. I remembered the original amount of the check and watching Dad go through everyone who needed to be paid back or paid finally.

It was that moment that I finally understood. Dad worked to live and lived to work. For him, providing was the name of the game. It was his sole purpose. Being a provider was both a privilege and a responsibility to him as a man. Not being able to provide the basic essentials for his family, was his biggest fear. To suppress that fear, he worked. Always.

The Extraordinary Lesson: Be known for your strong work ethic & sacrifice.

It wasn't that Dad didn't want to come to my games or spend time with me or take me to cool places. It was the fact that he had to put in the hours for our survival. I didn't know that sometimes he worked on jobs that didn't give vacation time with pay. I didn't know that he worked overtime intentionally, knowing he was tired and needed rest, for extra pay so that he could pay off tabs or pay back loans that he took to help us stay afloat through rising bills and other costs. This wasn't about me at all, but at the same time, it was definitely about me.

If Dad didn't do anything right, he was going to always make sure he was working and could afford to keep his family together with all that we need. Sometimes that meant sacrificing time and opportunity, but that was his work ethic, and he was never afraid to make the sacrifice for us. He came from a generation of men who's whole identity surrounded around taking care of your family and working harder than the next person to make sure that your table keeps food on it and the roof stays over your family's heads. That was it. Personal ambitions were secondary. Not by force, but by choice.

On another note, Dad recognized the value and importance of letting your work ethic speak for you. Your work ethic will speak for you before you open your mouth to say what you can do. Your work ethic will have your name spoken in rooms you haven't stepped foot in yet. Your work ethic is your professional reputation. You should work diligently to preserve it, build it, and protect it.

"Lemme' get 2-4-3 FIFTY / FIFTY BOX."

~~~~~ ∞ ~~~~~

Dad [to clerk]: ***Lemme' get 2-4-3 fifty-fifty box.***

Me: *Dad, what does that part mean when you say, "fifty-fifty box"?*

Dad: *Huh?*

Me: *When you gave him your number you said, "fifty-fifty box." What does that mean? How does that help you win?*

Dad: *Oh, it means I can win whether it comes 2-4-3 or 4-3-2 or 3-4-2 which ever kinda way.*

Me: *Oooohh... I would do 6-1-7 fifty/fifty box.*

Dad: *Yeah.... You don't wanna play this when you get older. It's a bad habit. Real bad. I wanna quit every day but.... I just can't. I will one day. But you don't do this, understand?*

Me: *yes sir.*

Sometimes, the lesson isn't always plain, clear, or even direct. This was one of those, *"do as I say and not as I do"* moments. But this was different. This wasn't like the usual no smoking or no drinking conversation, this was about winning millions and being financially comfortable for life! It was a lifestyle that people from my circle only daydream about having. So, to me when Dad says don't do it, I'm thinking why not? You play to win, and you win sometimes. Why wouldn't I want to take my shot? It can't be that hard to guess a few right numbers.

Well at this moment I couldn't play because I was only 11. However, Dad had been living in this world of gambling for years on years. He's seen more valleys than he's seen mountaintops in this game of lottery. There was way more to this than what I knew at that time. Including the psychological and financial impact it can cause.

The psychological impact is the hardest one to control. Often, it controls you. In this case, it's the constant yearning to win. You can never be satisfied. No one wins one time and says, *"great, I did it… I'm done now."* It's like any other addiction. An addiction doesn't always mean drugs. You will keep yearning for the thrill and in this case the thrill comes whether you win $40, $400, or $400,000,000. The thrill comes when you're one number off or you might have second guessed your original plan and can't help but to wonder now if you had just played a six instead of a four, you'd be millions of dollars richer right now.

And the cycle continues. Until a drastic situation forces you or you proactively seek assistance to wean off of the addiction. Again, no different than being addicted to heroin, cigarettes, pornography, or alcohol. The only difference, a different carrot is being dangled in front of you.

For Dad, the psychological had different variables. It wasn't just about becoming rich; it was also about escaping poverty. It was about eliminating debt in the quickest way imaginable. The allure of knowing that one day you could just simply spend $1 and that turns into winnings of $1,000,000. That's a thrill! That's a chance that most are willing to take. It really gets the endorphins in our mind going non-stop.

Nevertheless, the addiction was crippling and serious. Dad knew this all too well, and Mom did too. Dad and Mom were known to be inseparable. As they say, where you see Pop, there's Gloria… and vice versa. Most times, the two of them together would mean they're not too far from a lottery line.

They had quite a system going for themselves. The way they studied and prepared for this night in, and night out was very calculated. It was almost as if they had a degree in numerical engineering. There were magazines, scrap paper everywhere with numbers on them being cross referenced to previous weeks, months and years. They had this down to a science and memorization to the point where they could tell you the last time a specific pick 3 or pick 4 number was played in that same sequence or not. You'd think with all of this mathematical engineering, codebreaking and analytical equation work going on, winning would be like second nature.

Unfortunately, that's not how the game is played.

One time, they actually won big. Big enough for Dad to buy a car. Our days of having no car and having to borrow or rent a car had finally come to an end. I didn't have my license yet, but I too could feel the relief of that win. As much as it meant to our family to finally have a car and be able to do things and go places as a family, it also meant that Dad could get to the lottery line quicker to play yet again… and again.

As exhilarating as that win was, it was preceded by weeks, months, and years of not winning big, or at all. To some, that may seem like it's not a big deal and that we should keep being persistent with the opportunity. Here's a simple way to see how insurmountable this can become:

$1 = One number played (i.e. 2-4-3 fifty-fifty box)

You play that number, along with about 14 other number sequences that you feel good about, daily! That now equals $15 per day.

There are 365 days are in a year.

So, let's multiply that number by the $15… and you'll get an annual cost of $5,475 a year spent on the hope of trying to win millions.

Now, imagine all that could have been done with $5,475 in a year. For the sake of conversation, let's say that the year is 1995. I'll give you an idea of what that could have covered:

- *The fees and cost of equipment for me to play youth football with my cousins*
- *Two pairs of name brand shoes so I wouldn't get teased in school*

- *The down payment on a pre-owned vehicle so we could stop needing to catch the bus*
- *A washer and dryer for the home so we wouldn't have to go to the laundromat anymore*

…and after all of that, there would probably still be about $1,000 left over.

As if that was detrimental enough, one day, trouble hit home. Trouble as in the financial ramifications. I learned a lot by eavesdropping on closed door arguments between Mom and Dad. Anyway, the addiction to gambling and playing lottery would get the best of Dad to the point where he would "gamble to gamble." What I mean by that is Dad would take a chance at spending some of the rent money he's been saving for the month, just to play his lottery. His plan (or hope) was that he would make the money back before the rent is due by working an extra few hours here and there or by way of "hacking" (the unofficial Uber/Lyft service of Baltimore). This did not work. In fact, it hardly ever worked the way Dad planned. But this one time, it not only didn't work, but his plan B also, did not work.

The worst part about it all, Mom found out and when she found out, all hell broke loose. She was under the impression that Dad had the bill money separated from the leisure money. However, Dad had gambled on that process to fulfill his need to play his favorite numbers yet another day. Well this time, consequences fell.

They argued for at least an hour back and forth. They played the blame game and brought up past transgressions from almost ten years ago, to just ten minutes ago. Mom's position was about the responsibility part. She was under the impression that he had everything separate like it once was. She spoke mostly about the money loss, but that shifted quickly. It had stop being about the money and started being about family and Dad's responsibility to maintain our home and needs. His incessant need to play lottery and other gambling games interfered with his ability to take care of his first priority, our home. The home that sheltered his wife and kids, is what he really gambled with. I learned that day exactly what those folded up yellow notes were that I had seen taped on our front door for years. They were reminders of Dad's addiction.

The Extraordinary Lesson: Self-control and discipline breeds wisdom.

I learned a couple of things in that. First, hiding financial decisions in a marriage is a huge no-no. But also, the addiction to gambling is no less of a strong hold as an addiction to cocaine or heroin. Once you've had a taste of winning or coming close to winning… or you just feel strongly about your ability, you're hooked. In a bad way if you can't exercise control. I've never gambled in this way like Dad did. It's almost a fear that I have to lose what I can't control. I can't control what numbers pop up on that screen and the idea of losing money trying to guess just never sat well with me.

I remember going to Atlantic City once with some co-workers from my days working at Enterprise rent-a-car, and I remember wanting to play blackjack at a real blackjack table because until that point, I had only played for fun on a computer. We get there, and I go straight towards blackjack table. I at that moment learned that it was $10 just to sit at the table and get a hand dealt to you. Initially I'm thinking this isn't too bad. But then there were bets of no less than $100. I only had $100 to begin with! So, with the quickest agility I might have ever had, I got up from that table and was on my merry way. All I could think about was the stress and addicting power that lottery had on my Dad. That argument alone that I was eaves dropping on when I was younger, was enough to prove to me that didn't want or need to be anywhere near this gambling life. If I'm going to have an addiction, at least let it be to something with an immediate return on investment that doesn't cripple my health or wallet.

"Same thing, different name."

~~~~~ ∞ ~~~~~

Dad: *Whatchu think about these?*

Me: *[looking at the logo]: Nah, let me look some more.*

Dad: *What? Why not...? You said you wanted white high tops, didn't you?*

Me: *Yeah, I did but it's not those.*

Me [to the clerk]: *Do you have Air Force Ones?*

Clerk: *Not in this section.*

Dad: *They over there in that high price section?*

Clerk: *Yes sir. They just dropped. On sale this weekend for $109.*

Dad: *Shhiiiiiddd.... Carlos you need to stay right in this section here.*

Me: *Dad please? Everybody else wear Nike or reebok or New Balance. They make fun of people who don't! Makes me not even wanna go to school. Tired of getting laughed at.*

Dad: *Carlos I don't give a damn who laughin'. They ain't payin' for your shoes, I am. These shoes here ain't bad. They're the **same thing**, just a **different name!***

Me: *Ok.*

What else was I supposed to say? I was 13 years old, headed to the 8th grade, and not quite yet eligible to work and earn my own money. As much as Dad drilled in me that there's not much difference between the name brands, this was just as equally about the amount of money it cost to appease my "need" to have name brand shoes.

I've been down this road before though. The result was always an underwhelming one. My 'back to school' kicks were often "less desirable" by the standards of my peers. Now, I don't want this to seem as if I'm not grateful for my parents providing for me with what they could afford. I'm just saying, a name brand would save me from plenty of hard days in middle school. My shoe selections ranged from Pro Wings, to Roos, to Etonics, to Sauconys, and even All-Stars. All-Stars looked a lot like Chuck Taylor's

Converses, but were not and they were found everywhere Converses were not, like K-Mart. So, you would think I wouldn't care because I've been through this before.

No.

This time it was different. I felt different. I had reached a point was I had enough of the teasing in school. I was tired of being ashamed to put on my gym shoes and seeing everyone in Nikes, Jordans, Reebok Pumps, Penny Hardaways, Air Force Ones, etc. Meanwhile, I have something from Payless. I thank God for my cousin Aaron, who would give me a pair of his old shoes because he either outgrew them or just got a new pair. Either way, it was beginning to get to me. I wanted my own pair of name brand shoes, which were new, popular and mine. Why? Because having the newest shoes meant you were popular and being popular meant not being teased. Easy equation to me.

But to Dad, it wasn't about me and my popularity. My need to fit in with the cool kids was not at all a priority to him. It's like that line in Fresh Prince's song "Parents Just Don't Understand" where his Mom says, *"you go to school to learn not for a fashion show"*. That's basically what my Dad was saying to me in so many ways. To Dad, having name brand clothes and shoes just wasn't a thing of importance. To him, if you have clothes and shoes to put on, you are well taken care of.

He often reminded me of how he had less as a child and never complained about name brands. To me, I just felt like that's just how things was in the 60s, but this is the 90s. Also, unlike Dad, I didn't grow up with nine brothers and sisters, and clothes and shoes in the 90s were better than the clothes and shoes in the 60s. Deep down, I thought often about his method and position on this and if it was to be economically savvy, or if this was this Dad's way of saving money for other things important to him or us as a family. Regardless, this was an area where he would not budge.

Tough spot for a I'm 13 years old. I'm fighting for my acceptance and my Dad is literally ripping away any chance I have at that. I'm angry, resentful, and frustrated because I can see my opportunity at popularity and favor amongst the few girls who actually give me attention, just slipping away right before my eyes. But what can I really do? So, I accepted the reasoning because again, I can't afford to buy these things myself. Something was better than nothing at least.

Fast-forward to about 2008. At this point, I'm 25 years old, living on my own in a one-bedroom apartment, a college graduate with a relatively good job and of course, I now have bills. I have rent, a car payment, auto insurance, cable with internet service, gas and electric service, student loans, and I have to keep food in my house. Real life bills and responsibilities.

Then one day while I was going through my pile of bills, it reminded me of the same pile of bills that Dad used to keep on his dresser.

I'm sitting there and I'm seeing the bills, and I'm seeing a watch that I want. It was the Diesel DZ7333. Retail price $355.00. I had been collecting watches for about three years at that point and this watch had been on my watchlist (no pun intended) for months.

Then in that exact moment, I had this epiphany. I noticed how it all worked. Adulting has shown me how economics, commerce, and materialism work on our minds and our wallets.

We live in a capitalistic society. Everyone is competing, everyone has "the best and greatest and most exclusive" product or service. It's all a ploy to gain the upper hand on the consumers dollar. I'm the consumer, I have to be smart about MY dollar. How many times have you bought something or asked for something based on brand recognition or momentary trend, just to not be as excited about it three months later? Dad knew that and to him it was the "name brand trap." A trap that he refused to see me follow and surely refused to pay to see me follow it.

So, it made sense, later in life at least from the financial standpoint. But there was more to this lesson with Dad.

Beyond just the lesson of the value of the dollar, this was also a lesson about confidence. I'm more than sure that Dad's lesson or intention wasn't to teach me to be confident, but that's exactly what it did. Being a teen in the 90's going to school with shoes and clothes that wasn't name brand was a recipe for all types of bullying and ridicule. And I had my share of it. But through that, Dad still had a way of building up my confidence. When it came to being teased, Dad's response to that was simple:

"You need to learn to let that go in one ear and out the other."

Do you have any idea how hard that is at 13 years old?

It is extremely difficult to stand there and take bullying and verbal jabs and being the subject of ongoing jokes every school year. I mean they don't even forget it over the summer break! It's like the moment they see you again… they remember the jokes from last year and got new ones for this year.

Dad cared, but he didn't care. To him, it was just as easy as to declare, *"to hell with them!"* He'd tell me things also like, *"these are your clothes and shoes, they don't have to like them."* Or *"If you like it who cares if they do."* And probably my favorite, *"if they tease you, laugh with them. They only do it because they know it'll get to you. Once they see it doesn't bother you, then they look stupid."* That was a confidence booster.

P.S. It worked.

The Extraordinary Lesson: Materialism depreciates in value, and your character.

By force and involuntary agreeance, I learned to not get caught up in labels but focus on quality and to be both confident and content in what I have. People are going to laugh and ridicule until the end of humanity, but their power lies within your acceptance and being affected by their antics. Once you remove your care and concern, you remove their power to affect you.

As for the economic lesson here, it's very simple. Why pay twice the amount for something that's going to do the exact same thing as it's cheaper counterpart? To me, that made sense. Whether they were Jordan's or Pro Wings, I was going to wear them to gym class, play in them, get them dirty and then need a new pair in six months. Dad saved himself hundreds living by that rule. Now, I share that same value. Instead of wearing what's expensive, I rather make my bank account and IRA expensive.

However, that doesn't mean go through life cheating yourself of quality brand things. Just do so with wisdom. Does it appreciate or depreciate? Will you care about it with the same level of intensity in three months?

There was this quote I came across one day and it read:

"We buy things we don't need with money we don't have, to impress people we don't like."

If I didn't know that quote came from the world-renowned financial expert, Dave Ramsey, I would have sworn that it came from Dad.

"You gotta think three moves ahead."

~~~~~ ∞ ~~~~~

Me: *I don't know what to do.*

Dad: *I'm not gonna tell you. I see at least three things you can do.*

Me: *What are they? Tell me.*

Dad: *Nope.* [with a slight laugh]

Me: *Ahh c'mon Dad why not?*

Dad: [looks at me, says nothing]

Me: [thinking about options]

Dad: *You figure it out yet?*

Me: [attempting to do what I think makes the most sense]

Dad: *Nope!*

Me: *What? Why not?!*

Dad: *Because you gotta figure it out. Look over the whole board.* **You gotta think three moves ahead.** *You gonna have to earn this win.*

This could be interpreted in many different ways, but at that time, it was simply about the game of chess. This conversation took place during my first real game of chess. When I say, "first real game," I mean my first game where I felt ready to play on my own. Up until this point, I had learned how pieces move, some basic opening strategies, some beginner level defensive tactics and a couple of trick moves.

For a few months leading up to this game, I had been watching Dad play chess with guys in the barbershop while we waited to get our haircuts. I watched, I asked questions, I watched some more, then I asked to learn the game. For the next few months, on and off when Dad had a few moments to spare after dinner, he'd teach me how to play. The more I learned, the more I felt ready for my first test. That test being" the student defeating teacher." That's what this game was about for me. I had learned enough and had played checkers plenty before. As I seen it, it can't be that much different than checkers, right?

WRONG.

Chess was HARD. It wasn't a fast-paced game like checkers. It wasn't as easy as trading off pieces until there are no more left. It required a lot of thinking. Not just thinking for yourself, but subsequently anticipating what your opponent is going to do and basing your moves off those anticipations. All of that, while trying to plan your own attack. In your mind, is a constant struggle of "do I attack, or do I defend? Who do I move?" Every move was second guessed. Every thought I had for a move, was cancelled with "nah, that won't work". Eventually that led to my being scared to make a move because I didn't want to lose a piece. The anxiety of knowing that I could lose the game in five moves was frightening.

Aside from that, I was still very competitive. I wanted to win! I didn't want to be allowed to win just because I was in the learning stage. I wanted to show Dad that I had learned all he taught me, and I could beat him. Why? Because it's considered as a feather in the cap to defeat the one who taught you. That world be the pinnacle of reaching success.

So, as Dad and I are playing the game, he's doing things I haven't noticed before. Not on the board, but in general. As if he knew how to distract me and throw me off of my game. While we played, he would first test my honesty and walk completely away to see if I'd move a piece while he was gone. Or he would play "that old music" from the 60s and 70s. Now, I absolutely love and appreciate the R&B and funk of that era. However, at the time of playing chess, I don't want to listen to Flashlight by Parliament, anything by the Temptations, or Strawberry Letter 23 by the Brothers Johnson. Speaking of, why is it called Strawberry Letter 23, but in the song, they say Strawberry Letter 22? Did they miss a letter?

Another thing Dad would do, is talk to me throughout the game about random things. He would want to hold a full conversation about an old western TV show called

'Gunsmoke' or tell me a story about something he did in the old neighborhood with his brothers about 25 years ago. As strategic as he was, he only did this during my turn. I must say, it worked. In fact, that's something he's always done when we would play. I had to learn how to see that coming ahead of time. Once I learned his tactic, It became easy to return the favor with conversations about how Michel Jordan was better than Julius Erving or how the 2000 Baltimore Ravens defense was better than the Steel Curtain of the 70s.

Playing chess with Dad was about lessons. At first, the lessons were about the game. Learning how to move pieces and be strategic in those moves while thinking three moves ahead were all about the game.

It came to me later in life that Dad was teaching me life lessons all along through the game. Strategy, thinking before you move or act, being able to bounce back from a loss, and making sure every move you make has a plan B. In 2009, we started a

Father's Day tradition. A best of three chess series. The first series was when I realized what he had been doing all along. He was teaching me life through the game of chess.

The Extraordinary Lesson: It's not a loss if you learn, have patience, and have a plan. That's winning.

I learned three lessons through a not so simple game of chess. We've all heard the saying, "patience is a virtue." That's an old cliché that still rings true. But it's only true after you've practiced it and had to exercise patience in pressured situations. Some play the game of chess with a clock to teach you how to make quick, yet smart decisions.

Dad taught me how to play the game of chess without the use of a clock so that I would learn patience. It forced me to sit and wait for his move. Sometimes, he would already know what the move is he wants to make, but to test me, he'd take even longer. All the while I'm sitting there waiting and thinking. As time consuming as it was, that shaped my patience in life.

Some examples of how that the chess lesson of patience worked for me later in life include being patient when it comes to:

> ➢ *rush hour traffic*

> ➢ *being married*

> ➢ *working in Corporate America*

> ➢ *having a child*

Each one of them require patience. You can't make the cars on the road move any faster by yelling, flipping the middle finger, and angrily honking your horn. So, you have patience. Being married requires a type of patience that you likely didn't know you had. You have to master the art of understanding a whole human, which takes patience to have patience. Corporate America will test your patience with lazy employees, redundant practices, and spending your days giving your all while you wait for your opportunity to "climb that ladder." Having a child is work, and as a father parenting a child in a completely different generation than your own, surely requires patience. You need patience to understand their world even when you don't like something about it. You need patience to recognize that they are their own person, not a replica of yourself. So they will think differently, act differently, and respond differently.

Next, it was about the strategy. Or the simple art of planning and thinking ahead.

If you don't plan and strategize in the game of chess you will lose. There's no getting around that. Each piece has a specified range, movement and rule to it. Each piece can complement another piece. Each piece represents its' own power and ability and depends on the others to be effective. You must create your offense and defense with every move. You must examine every possible outcome of your opponent and prepare to counter every possible outcome. Before making a move, say to yourself (not aloud), *"How great is the risk if I make this move? Will I be in danger or set myself up for a successful attack? While at the same time, protecting my investments and assets?"*

Those same questions can apply to life.

In life, you can prepare better for tomorrow, when you look at all options and prepare for every possible outcome whether it's a test at school or a project at work or just something you're attempting for the first time. For me, it taught me to plan for three outcomes in everything: the best, the worst, and if nothing happens. That way I not only limit, but I control the way I react to any and almost everything.

Lastly, I lost to Dad quite often. When I was a child playing against him, he was throwing me a bone by taking it easy on me. That built up my confidence, but most times I was still taking a loss. That built up my character. The moment I would lose the game, Dad would say, *"Now let me show you what you did wrong..."*. It was as if he was already soothing my bruised, competitive ego ahead of time by immediately showing me where I went wrong and how to improve. He taught me that losing, is a lesson to be learned. It's not an opportunity to sulk and beat yourself up. It's a time for reflection, evaluation, recognizing the strengths and perfecting the weaknesses.

If you've heard the expression "Ball is Life," commonly used by basketball players, fans, and enthusiasts, then allow me to introduce to you a new one… *"Chess is life."*

"OPEN your mouth and speak!"

~~~~~ ∞ ~~~~~

Dad: [yells from across the aisle in Kay-Bee Toy store] *Carlos!*

Me: *Yes sir!?*

Dad: *C'mon over here!*

Me: [puts down the toys I want but won't ask for because I know the answer will be 'no']

Dad: *Come here. This is Mr. Darnell one of my good buddies from the neighborhood.*

Mr. Darnell: *Hello Carlos! Your father talks about you a lot.*

Me: [blank stare and slight wave]

Dad: *What you 'pose to say?*

Me: *Hello.*

Dad: *Just Hello??*

Me: *Hello Mr. Darnell.*

Dad: [to Mr. Darnell] *He must be ready to go...*

[Time passes very quietly. About an hour or so later, we get in the car]

Dad: [turns the volume down to the radio because he's about to talk] … *Carlos.*

Me: *Yes sir.*

Dad: *Don't you do what you did today ever again. You understand me?*

Me: *What did I do?*

Dad: *When an adult is talking to you, or anyone, **open your mouth and speak!** It's called respect. And if you don't show it, you won't get it. Do you understand?*

Me: *Yes sir.*

For me, this was one of those, "what's the big deal" moments. The way I had seen it, Mr. Darnell spoke, I waved because waving was my thing, and we were done. I didn't know Dad was so hellbent on me responding a certain way. To me, it felt rather militant as if Dad were a drill sergeant and I was Gomer Pyle. That's not to say that I was not a fan of showing respect, I just felt like the extra fanfare was a bit excessive. Is a wave not acknowledgment?

Dad did not care a bit about my perspective on the matter. It was about respect and as long as he was breathing and within arm reaching distance of me, he was going to ensure that I show a level of respect to others, especially my elders.

The more Dad talked to me about respect, the more I learned of what his expectation would be for me. This respect thing included more than just speaking. It was a matter of exercising good manners and being a gentleman. So in addition to opening my mouth to speak when someone greets me, Dad ensured that I learned how to do all of the simple gestures that mean something. The mannerisms that exudes and attracts respect. Things like making eye contact when greeting another adult, saying 'yes ma'am' and 'yes sir'; never responding to a question or call with the word, 'what', saying 'please' and 'thank you', and putting 'mister' or 'miss" in front of the name of an adult.

It once got to a point for me where I felt like I had to catch my every move. After constantly being told how to address adults, I was afraid to disappoint Dad. For many reasons, one of which being a whoopin'. But mostly, I believed everything he told me was right in some sort of way. Even if I didn't agree with it. That too was something he said to me one day:

Dad: *You might not like what I'm tellin' you, but you need to understand that it's for your own good. I'm your father, I'll never steer you in the wrong direction or tell you to do something that's bad. My father didn't do it to me, and I believed everything he's said to me to this very day. And he's been gone for years now. I expect the same outta you, ok son?*

Me: *Yes sir.*

I started being very intentional at a young age with all of these 'Rules of Respect'. Then I noticed that even at a young age, it was paying off. I was beginning to be differentiated from others. Being seen as a very respectable young man and often hearing, *"you raising him right, Pop. Keep it up! He's gonna be a fine young man when he grows up!"*

If I'm being totally transparent, I actually liked the attention. I liked the distinction that exercising these manners and rules of respect bestowed upon me. It gave me a sense of pride in how I carry myself and how others viewed me. Suddenly this didn't seem like a chore, but more like a way of life. Maybe this wasn't a bad thing after all.

Ok. Life goes on, and of course I heard that same saying from Dad again, but this time in a not so bad situation.

Dad: *You ready?*

Me: *Yup!*

Dad: *Alright! Gonna knock 'em dead son-son!*

Me: *Yeah, I hope I will. I think I will.*

Dad: *You'll be fine. Remember, firm handshake, look them in their eyes,* ***open***

your mouth and speak...no mumbling or half-ass answers and smile. You'll be fine. Ok!?

Me: *Got it.*

That was a pep-talk before my interview for my first job. I was interviewing to become a Crew Member at McDonald's. Dad knew me well because he knew my nervousness would make me give one-word answers, stutter when nervous, and mumble. But this pep talk and these basic tips, gave me a sense of confidence. It gave me a confidence to go into that interview, lead in with a handshake, maintain direct eye contact (especially with speaking and answering questions), and being conversational in my responses to questions. I was ready. I may have gone to that interview in a pair of slacks, one of Dad's shirts, a tie my grandmother handmade, and some square-toe oxfords from Payless ShoeSource, but the confidence that I was wearing that day was the best part of the outfit.

Respect and confidence are what came out of these talks with Dad. As a child, I used to view doing these things as another thing Dad was making me do. He was the type of father where you didn't question why he wanted you to do something, you just did it because he said so and because he said it was right. But when it came to this, he made sure I realized that when I became an adult, having respect for others and confidence in myself would be the key I need to go far in life. I must say, he was right.

The Extraordinary Lesson: Let there always be respect and confidence in your voice.

I had no idea how these small gestures would mean so much more in my life as a young man, and not so young man, a father, a husband, a co-worker, a mentor, a manager, and so many other roles that I've been blessed to hold. I didn't know at a young age how this lesson would translate into so many areas of life. A simple handshake with eye contact and speaking up clearly can make a world of a difference. It can make a difference in how you're perceived. It can be the difference maker between "I want to hire you" and "you don't seem like a good fit." Or, for the entrepreneur, it could be the difference between, "I want to fund your business project," or "that's nice keep up the good work." You owe it to yourself to build your character on the principles of respect and confidence. Don't be afraid to be set apart, even the number one is odd.

"*Nothing beats a fail but a TRY.*"

~~~~~ ∞ ~~~~~

Dad: *Hey son! How'd it go?*

Me: *It was fine. We came in 2nd. Fell short to the county boys again.*

Dad: *oh yeah. Well how'd you do?*

Me: *Ok I guess. I didn't do as good as I wanted.*

Dad: *Why you say that?*

Me: *Because I suck at high jump. I can do long jump, triple jump, hurdles, but I can't seem to make it over the bar for high jump.*

Dad: *Well what's the problem?*

Me: *It's the way I have to do it. I have to run and twist my body mid-air and go over the bar without touching it. It's too hard.*

Dad: *Well son,* ***nothing beats a fail but a try****.*

Me: *Whatchu mean?*

Dad: *You tried it, right?*

Me: *yeah and I failed at it.*

Dad: *But you tried it. So, you can never go through life wondering if you coulda or shoulda did it. You tried, you know it ain't your cup of tea, be proud that you gave it a shot and move on. I wouldn't have been able to do it either, I tell you that.*

I didn't know what to think here. The more I replayed what Dad said to me, the more it felt as if Dad just taught me how to be ok with failing. Which was rather difficult to grasp considering my competitive nature. As I seen it, I'm supposed to be good at everything I put my mind to. If I try it, I should be relatively good at it. So how could I possibly be ok with failing just because I tried? No one cares about a participation trophy. I surely do not when it comes to competition. A participation trophy to me just simply says that you showed up and did what you were asked with just enough effort to not be singled out for being the worst or last. In most cases, that's no different than punching the clock on time. Even as a teen and a young athlete, I knew that just showing up meant very little and, in most cases, just nothing more than a basic expectation. Needless to say, I walked away from that conversation a bit puzzled.

And then it hit me. The following week.

It was mid-January 1999. I had another track meet at the Fifth Regiment Armory. The armory had such a competitive aura in the atmosphere. It was the home of the Maryland National Guard, so perhaps that also gave it that competitive environment.

Nevertheless, I'm in there, warming up, scouting the competition across the gym and already calculating in my head who I'm likely going to be up against and how I intend to beat them. I was well-known for being the go-to-guy for any hurdling events and occasionally the 2nd or 3rd leg in any sprint relay races. That's what I was prepared for. But this time around, I was asked to step up and take on an event that was brand new to me. Coach asked me to do the high jump event. Now, this wasn't the first time he's asked me to do it, but it was the first time that I've accepted the challenge. Trust me when I tell you, I wanted so badly to say no and ask for a replacement. But in that moment, I had a realization. That realization was that if I turned it down again, that meant that I wasn't trying. I was failing because I gave it no effort.

I was already feeling competitive and hyped just from my own intended events. But now that I've had this realization, the competitive genes started to kick in even more. The competition wasn't who I could see across the track, but it was who I could see in the mirror. So, I amped myself up to take another shot at this high jump thing. I went over to the high jump pit and walked around the other participants with a cool and confident look on my face. As I circled them, I was studying their warmup routines, mimicking them so I look like I've been a professional at this high jump thing for some time now, all while psyching myself up for a triumphant attempt at redemption.

Then, the moment came. The moment where my name was called. I get to the line, making sure I'm positioned correctly with my toe right at the white line, I kneel a bit to get into the launch stance, and at the sound of the whistle, I take off, running full speed, adrenaline in my veins, ready to jump and clear this bar with ease like the professional I was just portraying myself as to the others.

I missed. I hit the pole. Three times. Not once did I clear it.

If I could have shrunk and disappeared, I would have in that very moment. I was feeling nothing but failure at that point. I felt as if I had not only let myself down, but I let my team, and I let my school down. Now, I'm taking that dreadful walk back to our sideline and I'm not at all in the mood for the team spirit thing where everyone is tapping you on the shoulder saying, "*good job,*" or "*you'll get 'em next time.*" While I'm sitting on the bench replaying where I went wrong, Coach Rev comes over to me with his marked-up clipboard and says, "*it's *alright Avent we're still in good shape."* I asked him how is that because I probably placed last in that. Then he tells me:

> *"Well no not actually. You still participated, that's still points. Even if you're in last place. Forfeiting or a disqualification would have been zero points, or they would have taken points away from us in the next event. So, we're ok. Get ready for the hurdles, that's coming up after the 200."*

Lightbulb moment.

Now what Dad had been saying was starting to make sense. But I realized that there was a very fine line to it all. I realized that Dad was talking about effort more than he was just showing up to go through the motions of it all.

Like most of the things he's told me, that wasn't the last time I heard that one either.

Dad: *Hey Son! How'd it go? Did you get it?*

Me: *I didn't get it.*

Dad: *Ahh man. Why not?*

Me: *They said they liked me, but they needed someone who could get the job done immediately because they didn't have time to spend on training someone like me.*

Dad: *Oh, ok I get it.*

Me: *I don't. How much time do they think I need? I'm a quick learner it's not like I needed weeks to get it.*

Dad: *I know, you would've been good for that job too but that's their loss.*

Me: *I feel like it's my loss.*

Dad: *No, it's not. It's theirs. You gotta remember what's meant for you, will be for you and in the end,* ***nothing beats a fail but a try****.*

Me: *You always say that.*

Dad: *Well it's true ain't it? You tried your best and that's what matters. You either take what you learned or whatever it was they said you ain't know how to do and go learn how to do it. Or leave it alone and let it be water under the bridge. That's up to you. But you fail when you do nothing. You're trying, and God sees it. Your turn is coming son, trust me. Don't even worry about it.*

I really wanted that job. And in that particular moment, Dad's words went over my head because I wanted to stay in my moment of feeling down. This was a good time for me to go to Mom too because she would tell me what I wanted to hear. What I wanted to hear was normally her telling me how sorry they'll be for not hiring her baby boy. I wanted to hear that, but I didn't need to hear that. So what Dad shared with me, stuck with me. It stuck to the point where it made me realize that failing is only failing when you don't learn anything from it and give up without giving yourself the chance to improve and try again.

P.S. I never attempted high jump again after that, but I did get better at hurdles. Also, that company doesn't exist anymore so perhaps, yet again, Dad was right.

The Extraordinary Lesson: Effort is your personal deposit into success.

Whether it was my attempts at the high jump or me going for a "dream" job, one thing I could say was that trying, and perseverance was present. I tried the high jump, and my effort counted. It was more effort than there would have been had I been disqualified or forfeited because I didn't want to do it. Now, of course I would have loved to have cleared the bar and earned at least a top three placement, but that's what the next time is for.

However, this lesson was bigger than track & field. It was about everything else in life. There's no failure when you give it effort. I noticed that more when I went out for the "dream" job. It might have seemed like everything I wanted but perhaps it just wasn't for me, and the lesson really was to learn from the disappointment, so that I can improve myself for the next opportunity.

You either win and see success, or you learn lessons to either improve the next time around or adjust your approach. The lessons become the blueprint to either win the next time or learn that you gave it your all and it's time to move on to the next challenge. That goes for sports or any aspect of life.

"I'm your DADDY, but He's your Father."

Me: Hey Dad?

Dad: Yeah.

Me: How come when we're in church, everyone calls God the father and they say, 'my father' or 'our father'? And who's the mother?

Dad: [slight chuckle] Because God is our father who art in heaven.

Me: I read that part, but how is he everyone's father? Aren't you my father? How can I have two fathers?

Dad: [laughs] No son you have one father on earth, me, and another in heaven, that's God.

Me: So that means it's two then, right?

Dad: Look at it like this, **I'm your daddy, but He's your father.**

Me: I don't get it.

Dad: God is all of our spiritual father. But on earth he gives some of us the chance to be a father on earth in the living form. So, *yes in a way you can say you have two fathers, but you have to know the difference and why you're saying that. That's why the Lord's prayer says, 'Our father which art in heaven'. That's the difference. And guess what, you can go to God and talk to God just as easy as you come and talk to me.*

Needless to say, this was very confusing to me and my young earthly mind. I walked away from this conversation thinking to myself:

> *"Is Dad my father or my brother in Christ or both? What about my Mom? What about when I want a girlfriend? Does that make her my sister too? I don't want that! How does this really work?"*

I needed answers. So, I did what I thought was the best thing to do, go to the source. I read my children's bible for two weeks straight, looking for answers or some sort of clues to explain what Dad said to me. My research didn't last too long because trying to read the bible in King James Version at 8 years old was a difficult task. Although what Dad said really puzzled me, it also was intriguing to think that this omnipresent being, whom I can't see, can't hear, and can't touch, was the father of all people and worthy of complete trust. The craziest part of it all, this being we call God our father, loves us all, knows all, and is everywhere. The thought of it all gave me the vibes of a superhero more than a father. Which to me, was a cool thing, but it didn't exactly solve the "how is he my father too" mystery.

Eventually I stopped challenging it and accepted it. I have an earthly father and a spiritual father. That can't be a bad thing, so I just let it be. But then I moved on some other burning questions, such as:

> *"How do I communicate with my father?"*
>
> *"Is praying the same as talking?"*
>
> *"Will I hear him?"*

> *"Do I have to use the kind of words that are in this weirdly written King James bible?"*

I saved these questions for the next time I could ask Dad. The more burning question for me was the one where I needed to know how to communicate with my father. I asked Dad once night while we were walking back home from Big Ma's house, and I was completely shocked by the answer. Dad basically said to me that I could talk to God just the same as I talk to him. I thought he was joking initially, like how could it be ok for me to talk to this superhero being in the same way that I would talk to my earthly, ordinary Dad?

Nevertheless, that's what Dad said, confidently and proudly. That more than enough assured me that he must be right. So knowing that, it took away some of my worries about how a prayer should sound. In the few times I've been to church up until this point, I've only seen and heard of prayers being performed in either a corporately structured way with a lot of those King James words being used, or a rather mumbling type of delivery of a prayer. So, this was good for me because I didn't quite know all of the big and difficult King James words to say to make sure my prayer was good enough for God to accept it and hear me.

While I was trying to learn more about this superhero figure we call God, Dad was preparing himself for a moment that would change his life.

It was November of 1991. We as a family didn't attend church often because Dad worked on most Sundays, and we didn't have a car. But one thing that was for certain, we would find out way there on the major holidays. On this particular night, it was the Thanksgiving week service. To me, it was just another one of those moments where we all end up in church because Big Ma or Grandma insisted that we come. However, this time was different. This was the night that Dad decided to officially turn away from his two decades long addiction to alcohol and give his life to Christ. What motivated this sudden change? Well, there were a few factors, but the one that I know meant the most to him was Mom telling him that he needed to either get his life together, or she was done with him. One thing about Mom, she means everything she says, no threats, always promises. Dad knew that, and he moved accordingly.

Okay, let's go back to that night.

I'm there with Dad and I'm sitting to his left, Mom is on his right. Everything was per the usual, and then something caught my attention. Dad is crying with his hands lifted, head lowered and appears very remorseful, but with joy. At this point, I'm watching him with such intent and awe, that I stopped playing with my Teenage Mutant Ninja Turtles and began trying to piece together what was happening in the moment. The next thing that I know, Dad gets up and starts walking towards the front of the church. Then, he turns back and signals for me to come with him.

Without hesitation, I go. I didn't know what was happening, but I knew that going anywhere with Dad was an adventure at eight years old. It didn't matter if it were Grandma's house, liquor store, or the laundromat. To me, as long as I can tag along, I was ready for whatever was ahead of us. So, this was no different.

But it was actually very different.

I had no idea that Dad was headed to the sacred space known as the altar, the front of the church. I was excited and curious because I had never been that close to the front before, and I wanted to see what it was like to be up there. In that moment, I didn't know that Dad was giving his life to Christ... and committing me with him. He wasn't committing me like Abraham sacrificing Isaac, but he took me with him as in wanting me to be saved with him. This was the beginning of me learning who God is. This was the pivotal moment where I was beginning to understand the whole concept of God being my father. The way that moment went, the public adoration, the spiritual glow that was amongst the church, it was really making sense to me. Dad had a look of relief on his face. Like he was finally able to shake something off of his back and reverence in the love and support of his "father."

Watching Dad through that experience, and how he was changed thereafter, helped me learn of this new "father" in my life who wasn't really new, but proven to be an all-powerful being that knows and loves me.

As the days went on after that pivotal night at church, Dad would spend almost every night thereafter at the dining room table, where he'd read his bible before and after dinner. Eventually he'd tell me to come to the table and bring one of my children bible story books. I had about 40 of them. The first time I sat with him, I noticed Dad putting those table of contents tabs on the edges of the paper of his bible, so he can find the books of the bible quickly. Something about seeing him do that showed me that he was serious about his newfound walk with God.

So, that became the thing for Dad and me. He and I having dining room table bible reading sessions a couple of times per week. As I would read the children-friendly version, Dad would read the bible King James version and we'd talk about what we've discovered. In all those conversations, it always came back to God and His omnipresence and how much he loves me as my father in heaven, as much as Dad did as my father on earth. Then he'd ask me questions about what I just read to see if I understood, and how what I just read, despite it happening 2,000 or more years ago, it could still relate to me in real time, in real life.

It was astonishing to me to know that this powerful superbeing was always there with me and for me. That was exciting because it was like having direct access to a superpower. That's how Dad got me to understand who God is and how God is my "father."

The Extraordinary Lesson: God hears you, sees you, and is always with you.

Dad and I had so many conversations about God and the bible. Especially in the beginning of his spiritual journey. But as I mentioned before, the greatest takeaway that I got from them all, was knowing that I can talk to God the same way that I talk to Dad. The concept of prayer doesn't have to be complex.

The older that I got and the more entrenched I became in my own spiritual journey, I struggled with not knowing if I'm supposed to pray with certain words, a certain tone, or a certain dialect. Which then led me to wondering if in my own relationship with God if it was strong enough. But remembering Dad's words reminds me often that my relationship with God, shouldn't make me feel inadequate because of words I use or a specific tone. But rather one of an intimate truth, like I would have with Dad.

"Be BETTER than me."

∼∼∼∼∼ ∞ ∼∼∼∼∼

Dad: *Carlos...... guess what?*

Me: *What?*

Dad: *[points to a high-rise senior building in northeast Baltimore] Built dat building!*

Me: *You did? By yourself?*

Dad: *Yup!*

Me: *[shocked silent look on my face]*

Dad: *Jack up boy! I ain't do it by myself. I used to work construction.*

Me: *You did? When?*

Dad: *Back in the seventies. Around seventy-seven, I think.*

Me: *Wow! You did construction before you started working in the market?*

Dad: *Yup and I used to work at the steel plant too. Drove trucks, worked forklifts, all dat dere boy!*

Me: *That's crazy! I wanna be like you when I grow up.*

Dad: *Nah no you don't.*

Me: *Why not? You had all of the cool jobs.*

Dad: *Nah you don't be like me; you **be better than me.** You'll go to college, get you a job where you don't have to just use your hands, but you can use your brains. Climb the ladder to the top. Make good decisions. That's what you gonna do because you're intelligent. Way smarter than me. Aight?*

Me: *Ok.*

Hope. Confidence. Validation.

That's what that conversation meant to me. From that moment, I started thinking about the future me. I didn't know where'd I go to college or if I'd even get in college, but I was confident that I would do something. The very fact that Dad told me to be better than him, meant to me that he seen more in me than I seen in myself at that time.

Although in that moment, I simply seen it as he just wanted me to get a good job. But as the years passed, I learned there was more in that statement than just getting a good job. It was about making the right life decisions. It was about being smarter and thoughtful in my journey in life and avoiding being care-free about life. There were paths he never wanted me to take and roads he never travelled that he wanted to see me travel.

He wanted me to be stronger than him, be taller than him, make better decisions than he did, and become more than average. He wanted better for me, and it was my job to execute that. Likewise, it was also Dad's vulnerable, self-aware way of insuring that the mistakes he made growing up, aren't repeated by me. He didn't get a 4-year college degree, he didn't go into the career that he had hoped for originally, he became hooked on alcohol, and it impaired some of his most critical life choices.

Dad knew that I had already seen different versions of him. I had seen the workaholic, I had seen the alcoholic, I had seen the gambler, I had seen the trying father, I had seen the struggle. I had seen how he'd not buy himself anything to make sure there was food in the house and clothes for me and my siblings. I had seen him borrow his brothers' car, so he could take me where I needed to go. All of this I had seen, and he wanted me to be better than it all. He lived and learned, and in that learning moment, he knew he had to make certain I didn't become him but become better than him.

He knew the road some of my friends were headed towards. He knew that an addiction to gambling could become of me if he didn't intervene at my earliest stage of inquisition. He knew that peer pressure could easily ride me into a life of alcoholism, just as it did him in his adolescence. He knew that I needed to have a relationship with God at an earlier stage in my life.

He knew that if I had any chance to survive in this city, this country, this world, I had to start by being better than him.

The Extraordinary Lesson: Always strive for better.

There's nothing stronger in a child's life than the encouragement from a parent.

It builds a level of confidence and assurance like nothing else could. A son needs his father to be a blueprint to life, while at the same time showing him how to live, love, and learn. The same rings true for a Mother and son, mother and daughter, or a father and daughter. But in my experience, I was a son who needed and benefited greatly from his father's presence and push to see me be my best version of me.

There is always better to achieve. There will always be room to improve. Never become content in one place. Take heed the lessons learned of those before you. Pave a way for those who will follow you. Stand out or someone else will stand in front of you. Every goal is meant to be met and once met, it's time for a new goal. Just as much as Dad wanted me to be better than him, I too wanted to be better than I was the day before, month before, or year before. Nothing handed, everything earned. There's something very satisfying about that, and Dad ignited me with that very statement.

THE EPILOGUE:

Every *story* has an *origin*

Dad: *You might not like what I'm tellin' you, but you need to understand that it's for your own good. I'm your father, I'll never steer you in the wrong direction or tell you to do something that's bad. My father didn't do it to me, and I believed everything he's said to me to this very day. And he's been gone for years now. I expect the same outta you, ok son?*

Me: *Yes sir.*

My father was doing what he knew was best. He was doing what he learned from his father, my grandfather. A man that I've only ever heard stories about, seen in pictures, and heard his name referenced, but I never met him. Yet here I am, being raised by his son and learning mannerisms, values and morals that preceded me by 60+ years.

That is a form of generational wealth.

Dad was one to make sure that he came across as deliberate and intentional, though sometimes they were indirect. But all the time, I knew that there was a meaning behind it and eventually I did realize that he did it all out of his love for me. Did I always understand the reasons and lessons the first time, no. And not even on the second time. That's what growth and learning is all about. But once I did get it, each lesson stuck with me for life. From my teenage years to my young adult years and so forth.

A defining moment that led me to back to thinking about my experiences with Dad and how they have shaped me into who I am, came to me through an exercise on values and lessons that I did during a two-day workshop with Gallup's Strengthsfinder. If you've never heard of it, I'd say it would be a very wise and inexpensive investment in yourself. Strengthsfinder is a self-help book and assessment by Don Clifton, which focuses on your innate strengths as a being. There are 34 strengths or talents that we all possess, but our top five are the ones that we just naturally act on daily. When I did this assessment, I discovered my top five to be the following:

Analytical – *seeking facts and details*
Competition – *comparing to improve*
Responsibility – *trusted to lead; ownership*
Significance – *independent, desire to impact*
Maximizer – *transforming good to great*

Now, when I first seen this, my reaction was more of *"ok, I see how I do that one, ok I know where that one is most noticeable, yeah definitely a lot of that in my day-to-day."* But then I thought about where these could have originated, and it was in that moment that it all turned into a full circle moment for me. Each of these strengths in their own way, took me back to one of these conversations that cumulated into a lesson from my Dad. Whether the strength was something I learned from him, observed from him, or he taught me to be, there was a direct correlation to him. In that moment, it made sense to me. It was as if I am the tree, my strengths are my branches, and Dad was the roots. These strengths were built in me over time by my father.

If nothing else, I hope that my experiences and my ordinary Dad's simple words, would prove to be impactful in one way or another. Maybe it's not today, maybe it is. Whenever that day is, I feel confident enough to say that Dad would only want the best for you and for you to always strive to be the best you. He gave me some timeless extraordinary lessons and I always say, what good is it to have knowledge, and not share it? I dare not take my own advice.

So with that said, I leave you with some encouragement, some food for thought, some motivation, and some genuine love that comes from a place that wants to see you amplify your best self through whatever circumstance you may be facing. As a father now, and a mentor to others, I'd say:

BE TODAY, WHAT TOMORROW NEEDS.

Be today, who your younger self needed yesterday.

Learn from your mistakes as well as your successes.

Try always and you'll never have regrets.

HUMILITY IS HONORABLE.

Confidence is essential.

KNOWLEDGE IS EVERLASTING.

Love is a powerful responsibility.

ABOUT the Author

~~~~~ ∞ ~~~~~

Carlos J. Avent is an educator, college & career counselor, youth development professional, and a best-selling author. A native of Baltimore, MD, Carlos is an alumnus of the third oldest public high school in the United States, the Baltimore City College. He then graduated from one of the nations' most prominent Historically Black Colleges & Universities (HBCU), Morgan State University, where he earned his Bachelor of Arts in Sociology. His educational journey continued with Walden University where Carlos earned his Master of Science in Higher Education and Post-Baccalaureate certification in Instructional Design. In 2019, Carlos earned the honor of being inducted into the National Society of Leadership and Success.

Carlos love for writing and storytelling began with a college course in creative writing and writing projects on social psychology, behaviorism, relationships, and social theory. Since then, additional projects and opportunities have included theater script writing, contributing writer of various K-12 and higher education newsletter and online publications, including the National Alliance of Public Charter Schools discussing the school choice debate, and Study.com to discuss first-year college success. One of his favorites was a critic review of the nationally toured stage play turned movie, "A night in Miami" in 2016.

Other writing opportunities included being a featured sports blogger, covering the Baltimore Ravens for online sports publications/websites, Fansided and Fox Sports. In 2020, Carlos co-authored The Black Father Perspective. This work includes a collection of essays written by Black fathers from all walks of life, coming together to share wisdoms, loving moments, and to dispel the myths of black fatherhood in America.

In the space of youth development, Carlos has served as a youth mentor and/or a program manager for various organizations/institutions such as Laureate Education, Inc., Collegebound Foundation, Morgan State University Alumni Association, Baltimore City College Alumni Association, and MENTOR MD | DC.

By profession, Carlos is a well-respected advisor and practitioner in higher education where his expertise is in college readiness, adult learning, instructional design, learning styles/metacognition, and strategies that support student retention and student success.

If you're looking for Carlos on social media world, look no further. Here's how you can connect:

facebook.com/carlosjavent

@carlosjavent

@carlosjavent

linkedin.com/in/carlosjavent

@carlosjavent

www.ingramcontent.com/pod-product-compliance
Lightning Source LLC
Chambersburg PA
CBHW081952110426
42744CB00031B/1899